Soaring Prayers

To Rev. Howard

God's Blessings

+ Speed to life

Ben D. John
Hallett

Soaring Prayers

Rev. Dr. John R. Halbert

To order additional copies of this book, contact:
Xlibris Corporation
1-888-795-4274
www.Xlibris.com
Orders@Xlibris.com
74983

I would like to dedicate this book to my wife
—Mae Halbert

Introduction

Most books published today assume that the majority of people can and know how to pray. My heart goes out to those who do not know what prayer is or how it works. Prayerfully, this book will help those who are seeking to learn the aspects of prayer. Prayer is simply communicating with God.

There are other aspects of communicating with God but for the purpose of this project we are going to use prayer.

This book is an attempt to outline each part of prayer and give examples of each part. The writing section allows you to create each part in your own words. Your words will help develop your confidence.

Each step is described for clarity. However, all parts are not necessarily needed to pray. But, each part can help you develop your ability to pray fervently and effectively.

There are also examples of Biblical characters who prayed and the results of their prayers. Select a character as your mentor.

This practice can also enhance the quality of those who are well experienced in praying.

Congratulations on your honest desire in taking the first step toward reaching a solution in learning how to pray.

John Halbert

Prayer Project for Beginners

The church is a ministry meeting the needs of its participants. The foundation for this ministry cannot be established firmly until it has been equipped with prevailing prayer. It cannot reach heaven high until it has met our earthly needs. These sessions on prayer are designed to motivate and encourage the believers to enrich their prayer life.

The following exercises are an attempt to help, assist, and guide anyone who is apprehensive about praying. They also can help those who want to pray effectively, (James 5:16 . . . The effectual fervent prayer of a righteous man availeth much.).

Everything and every form may be modified to meet your specific needs or situations. This is not an attempt to tell you how to pray but these proceedings can be used as a springboard to enrich your prayer life.

If you do not know how to pray or pray publically, this is an excellent start. Even if you are a veteran prayer, these exercises can make your prayer life stronger.

SESSION #1

Let's Begin: Please follow each instruction and complete each exercise.

The first and foremost hurdle to overcome and manage is the truth about self-concerning your ability to pray. Being honest in all communication with God and others is a necessary component of prayer, (Romans 12:17b . . . Provide things honest in the sight of all men.). If you are not willing to be serious and honest, there is a good possibility your prayers will not be effective. **Fill our form A** to remind you of your commitment.

Form A—Honest/Commitment.

STEP 1

Honest/Commitment Form A

I promise to be honest with all procedures in relation to this ministry. Therefore, I sign this form as a pledge of my commitment to be totally honest to God and myself with all my answers.

Sign: _____ Date: _____

Sign and read at least 3 times during these sessions.

SESSION #2

A pre-evaluation form has been provided as an attempt to focus on and an effort to measure your awareness about yourself, your ability to pray effectually. This form also surfaces your weakness and serves as a tool that will help measure your growth. This form may be modified to meet your needs or circumstances.

Fill-out the **Pre-Test form (Form B)**. Keep as a record and compare it with the post-test. Upon completion of this project, fill out the Post-Test form (Form B) to measure any growth.

Highlight or mark the most outstanding features or items that are a hindrance to your prayer life, remember **BE HONEST**. These items will help you develop your outline for discussion.

There are eighteen questions selected for the pre-test and post-test. These questions are designed to help discover your weakness. You have a choice of one of five responses to these questions. Circle the number that best fits you.

Response 1: ***NOT IMPORTANT***
Response 2: ***SLIGHTLY IMPORTANT***
Response 3: ***MODERATELY IMPORTANT***
Response 4: ***IMPORTANT***
Response 5: ***VERY IMPORTANT***

Key one   (1),   ***NOT IMPORTANT,*** meant that the person had no desire to know or learn about prayer.

Key two   (2),   ***SLIGHTLY IMPORTANT*** meant that the participant would be willing and interested in putting forth an effort to learn more about prayer.

Key three (3),   ***MODERATELY IMPORTANT*** suggested that this person's prayer life was such that they wouldn't pray until something happened and/or they wanted a favor from God.

Key four   (4),   ***IMPORTANT*** *meant* that prayer was already a part of their life, but they were willing to learn to pray more effectively. Finally,

Key five   (5),   ***VERY IMPORTANT*** indicated a person who was very mature in his or her own prayer life and expressed a willingness to help others learn to pray more effectively.

FORM B

Prayer Evaluation

QUESTIONNAIRE

__X__ (Pre-Test)
_____ (Post-Test)

The following explanations are guidelines for taking this evaluation. Please familiarize yourself with each numerical status prior to taking this evaluation.

1. *NOT AT ALL:*
2. *SLIGHTLY:*
3. *MODERATELY:*
4. *IMPORTANT:*
5. *VERY IMPORTANT:*

PLEASE SELECT A NUMBER (1-5) WHICH BEST DESCRIBES YOUR POSITION OR UNDERSTANDING OF THE FOLLOWING PRAYER ISSUES:

01. How interested are you in praying?	1	2	3	4	(5)
02. How interested are you in praying publicly?	1	2	3	4	(5)
03. How important is prayer in your life?	1	2	3	4	(5)

Question	1	2	3	4	5
04. How important is meditation in your prayer life?	1	2	(3)	4	5
05. Does fear affect your attitude toward prayer?	1	2	(3)	4	5
06. How influential are Biblical characters in your prayer life?	1	2	3	(4)	5
07. Does reading the Bible have a great impact on your prayer life?	1	2	3	4	(5)
08. Is prayer sufficiently incorporated into your life?	1	2	(3)	4	5
09. Is prayer a part of your daily routine?	1	2	3	(4)	5
10. Do you have direct goals and/or purposes in praying?	1	2	3	4	(5)
11. How important are the concerns of others to you when you are praying?	1	2	3	(4)	5
12. How confident are you that your prayers are being or will be answered?	1	2	3	(4)	5
13. Is it necessary for you to pray aloud versus silently?	1	(2)	3	4	5
14. Is it necessary to pray short prayers versus long prayers?	1	(2)	3	4	5

15. How important is it for you to use a certain format to pray?	1	2	3	(4)	5
16. How important is your prayer life to the growth of the church?	1	2	3	4	(5)
17. How essential are your prayers to the ministries of the church?	1	2	3	4	(5)
18. How much does your spiritual growth depend upon your prayer life?	1	2	4	(4)	5

Evaluate your answers and mark areas where improvement is needed.

.

SESSION #3

Section A

The facts about prayer to the beginner are that we don't know what prayer is, how to pray, what to say, how to say it, when to say it, where to say it, etc.

STEP 3

Discuss what prayer is and the parts of prayer.

Prayer is simply communication with God. Its parts may vary and may not occur in the order provided. The following outline provides an example of a complete prayer.

Normally there are 5 parts to a prayer:

1. Salutation/greeting
2. Thanksgiving/praise
3. Confession
4. Petition
5. Closing

A Brief Discussion on the parts of prayer

1. **Salutation/greeting** is important to know who you are addressing your prayers to. For an example: If a letter came to my house and did not identify who the letter was for, I would not perceive it was addressed to me. "After this manner therefore pray ye: Our Father . . .", Matthew 6:9.

    A. Write out your own salutation. _Father God in_

    Heaven .

2. **Thanksgiving/prais**e attempts to acknowledge the fact that God has Blessed you and you are grateful. As an effort to show Him your gratitude, you lift up praise unto Him. Lord I thank you. Bless your Holy Name. "One generation shall praise thy works to another, and shall declare thy mighty acts", Psalms 145:4.

    A. Bless your Holy Name.

    B. List two things you are thankful for. (1) _____

    _____ .

    (2) _____

    _____ .

3. **Confession** provides a channel to bring your faults and failures before God as an acknowledgment of your sins. "If we confess our sins, he is faithful and just to forgive us our sins, and to cleanse us from all unrighteousness. If we say that we have not sinned, we make him a liar, and his word is not in us", 1 John 1:9,10. "Confess your faults one to another . . ." James 16:1a.

    A. List two things you have done you feel are not pleasing to God.

       (1) _Fear and having doubt_

       (2) _____

4. **Petition** is simply asking God for what you need. "Be careful for nothing; but in every thing by prayer and supplication with thanksgiving let your requests be made known unto God. And the peace of God, which passeth all understanding, shall keep your hearts and minds through Christ Jesus" 'Philippians 4:6,7. Be specific.

    A. List two things you want God to do for you.(1) _Bless my ministry By Saving souls for Christ._

       (2) _Bless my Wife and Family_

5. **Closing** is a declaration on whose authority you are sending your prayers and who is sending it. "And whatsoever ye shall ask in my name, that will I do, that the Father may be glorified in the Son. If ye shall ask any thing in my name, I will do it", John 14:13,14.

     A. Create your own closing. *In Jesus Name* .

Write the sentences you have written in step 3 in their order.

_____

_____

_____

_____

_____

_____

_____

_____

Congratulation you have just written your first prayer.

SESSION #4

Section B

The Kinds of Prayer: There are two basic types of prayers.

1. **Private**—This prayer is consider as personal and is usually done alone.
2. **Public**—This is usually called cooperate prayer. It involves the interest of your audience along with your basic concerns." . . . Pray one for another . . . , James 5:16b. This prayer is usually prayed for an audience.

The significance of prayer is important. The desire to pray starts the adrenaline to flow and that depends on how motivated you are. The wrong motivation can hinder the answer of your prayers. The Pharisee and the sinner in Luke 18:10-13, "Two men went up into the temple to pray; the one a Pharisee, and the other a publican. The Pharisee stood and prayed thus with himself, God, I thank thee, that I am not as other men are, extortioners, unjust, adulterers, or even as this publican. I fast twice in the week, I give tithes of all that I possess. And the publican, standing afar off, would not lift up so much as his eyes unto heaven, but smote upon his breast, saying, God be merciful to me a sinner."

What motivated the Pharisee to pray? _____

_____.

Describe the motivation in the publican's prayer. _____

_____.

What is motivation?

Something that causes and encourages a given response. A basic for an action or decision. Something that encourages. There are three concepts that can help motivate you to pray: (1) Need courage to pray, (2) Need to be encouraged to pray, (3) Encourage yourself to pray.

1. Need courage to pray—Pray this prayer. Lord help me to pray.
2. Need to be encourage to pray—When I think of all the benefits God has given me, my soul cries out.
3. Encourage yourself to pray-You know your own needs better than anyone else.

List (10) things God has blessed you with. See form entitle Blessings.

Fill out **Blessing List Form C**.

FORM C

BLESSING LIST

List below some things you have in your possession that you didn't do anything to obtain it.

1. _____

2. _____

3. _____

4. _____

5. _____

6. _____

7. _____

8. _____

9. _____

10. _____

PRAYER

Father, I come to you with thanksgiving in my heart and praise upon my lips. I thank You for blessing me with these items above and that Your blessing will continue in my life. In the name of Jesus Christ. Amen.

By now your pre-evaluation form has been looked at. From your form, are there anything needing more discussion? Yes or No. If there are any, please go back and discuss them again. If not, then move further with the next session.

SESSION #5

The most common element to hindering prayer is fear. Fear paralyzes your prayers. Fear can invoke unbelief, which destroys the effect of prayer. In order to overcome you most hindrance element is to bring them to the surface and face them. Fear needs to be exposed to eradicate its effect in your life. Do not mistake Godly fear with fear. Godly fears encourages while fear discourages.

The only way to overcome fear is with the **WORD of GOD**. Jesus replied to Satan's tempts with the Word, "It is written . . ." The power in God's Word gives the victory to those who believe them. Below are some common fears. Yours may vary or be under another name.

Common Fears

1. **Fear of People**—Hebrew 13:6 So that we may boldly say, The Lord is my helper, and I will not fear what man shall do unto me. Matthew 10:28,

2. **Fear of Failure**—Philippians 4:13, I can do all things through Christ which strengtheneth me." Matthew 19:26; Mark 10:27.

3. **Fear of the Lack of**—Philippians 4:19 But my God shall supply all your need according to his riches in glory by Christ Jesus. Philippians 4:11

4. **Fear of Death**—Hebrew 9:27, And as it is appointed unto men once to die, but after this the judgment: 1 Corinthians 15:50-58.

5. **Fear of Sickness**-Exodus 15:26 And said, If thou wilt diligently hearken to the voice of the LORD thy God, and wilt do that which is right in his sight, and wilt give ear to his commandments, and keep all his statutes, I will put none of these diseases upon thee, which I have brought upon the Egyptians: **for I am the LORD that healeth thee.** Psalms 91:10: Luke 8:50

6. **Fear of Being Alone**—Matthew 28:I am with you always, even unto the end of the world. Hebrew 13:5, . . . said, I will never leave thee, nor forsake thee

7. **Fear of the Unknown**—Purposely left blank

8. **Fear of Betrayal**—Matthew 13:12, 13, Now the brother shall betray the brother to death, and the father the son; and children shall rise up against their parents, and shall cause them to be put to death. And ye shall be hated of all men for my name's sake: but he that shall endure unto the end, the same shall be saved.

9. **Fear of not knowing what to say**—Reread your blessing list along with step 3 section A

Jesus teaches us not to be afraid of anything. His words encourages us to be bold and trust in the Father through Him who gives us the victory over our fears.

"These things I have spoken unto you, that in me ye might have peace. In the world ye shall have tribulation: but be of good cheer; I have overcome the world," John 16:33.

For God hath not given us the spirit of fear; but of power, and of love, and of a sound mind. 1 Timothy 1:7,8

SESSION # 6

Writing Exercise

Exercise A: Rewrite several of the scriptures mention above making them personal using the phrase **It is written . . .** before each scripture. Example—It is written God hath not given **me** the spirit of fear; but of power, and of love, and of a sound mind.

_____

_____

_____

_____

_____

_____

_____

_____

_____

_____

_____

_____

_____

_____

_____

Remember when you begin to grow God will make opportunities for you to exercise your strengthen faith by allowing your faith to be challenge. Don't be afraid, just accept the quest and remember, It is written . . .

SESSION # 7

BIBICAL PRAYER PARTNERS

Prayer Partners:

Biblical characters in the bible you can and should identify.

Abraham—Genesis 12-18:22

John The Baptist—Luke 3:1-12; 7:18-25, John 1:1-34

David—2 Samuel 5-6

Deborah—Judges 4-5

Hagar—Genesis 16,21

Job—Job

Jonah—Jonah

Joseph—Genesis 37-50

Martha—Luke 1:38-42

Mary Magdalene-John 20:1-18

Moses—Exodus

Noah—Genesis 6-9

Onesimus—Philemon

Paul—Acts 9: 1-6, 22:4-16, 26:9-18
Peter—Matthew 16:15-23, 18:21-22, John 13:5-11, 36-38
Ruth—Ruth
Sarah—Genesis 17,18,21

The Assertive Widow B Luke 18:2-5
The Freed Woman B Luke 13:10-17
The Man Possessed by Demons B Luke 8:26-39

You may find others that meet your needs. Please list them and name your familiarity.

_____

_____

_____

If you were this biblical character, what would you be praying for? Praying about?

_____

_____

_____

_____

_____

Prayer partner covenant is a attempt to add a trusted person for added strength.

"For where two or three are gathered together in my name, there am I in the midst of them," (Matthew 18:20).

Please select your partner prayerfully. Sign two forms, one for your record and one for your partner.

Any part of this form may be modified for your usefulness.

PRAYER PARTNER'S COVENANT

We are joining in a prayer partnership

from_____

(Date)

To_____

(Date)

We agree to be faithful to the following items listed:

X   **Meet at least four times during the course of this project.**

X   Withhold judgment on problems or doubt communicated by our partner. Our attitude will be one of acceptability.

X   Avoid the temptation to try to solve each other's problems during these sessions. Our purpose for meeting is to pray.

X   Keep everything said at these meetings completely confidential. We must be able to trust each other if we are to develop openness between us.

X   Study the Bible five (5) times a week during the course of this project.

Signed, _____

SESSION # 8

Praying Expectantly

Write down five desires/needs. Take a few minutes, and then share them with your prayer partner. Offer a prayer for those needs. Show that you are ready to receive God's answer by holding your empty hands palms up when you pray or by holding each others hands.

PRAYER SENTENCES FROM SCRIPTURES:
PRAYER PROMISES

- Pray in the spirit at all times. (Ephesians 6:18)

- The Lord accepted my prayer. (Psalm)

- The Spirit intercedes with sighs too deep for words. (Romans 8:26)

- For He will hide me in His shelter in the day of trouble. (Psalm 27:5)

- Put your hope in God. (Psalm 42:5)

- Pray without ceasing. (1 Thessalonians 5:17)

- Come to me, all you that are weary and heavy laden, and I will give you rest. (Matthew 6:11)

- Give us this day our daily bread. (Matthew 6:11)

- The prayers offered in faith will make the sick person well. (James 5:15)

FORM B

Prayer Evaluation

QUESTIONNAIRE

_____(Pre-Test)
__X__(Post-Test)

The following explanations are guidelines for taking this evaluation. Please familiarize yourself with each numerical status prior to taking this evaluation.

1. **NOT AT ALL:**
2. **SLIGHTLY:**
3. **MODERATELY:**
4. **IMPORTANT:**
5. **VERY IMPORTANT:**

PLEASE SELECT A NUMBER (1-5) WHICH BEST DESCRIBES YOUR POSITION OR UNDERSTANDING OF THE FOLLOWING PRAYER ISSUES:ISSUES:

01. How interested are you in praying?	1	2	3	4	5
02. How interested are you in praying publicly?	1	2	3	4	5
03. How important is prayer in your life?	1	2	3	4	5
04. How important is meditation in your prayer life?	1	2	3	4	5
05. Does fear affect your attitude toward prayer?	1	2	3	4	5

06. How influential are Biblical characters in your prayer life?	1	2	3	4	5
07. Does reading the Bible have a great impact on your prayer life?	1	2	3	4	5
08. Is prayer sufficiently incorporated into your life?	1	2	3	4	5
09. Is prayer a part of your daily routine?	1	2	3	4	5
10. Do you have direct goals and/or purposes in praying?	1	2	3	4	5
11. How important are the concerns of others to you when you are praying?	1	2	3	4	5
12. How confident are you that your prayers are being or will be answered?	1	2	3	4	5
13. Is it necessary for you to pray aloud versus silently?	1	2	3	4	5
14. Is it necessary to pray short prayers versus long prayers?	1	2	3	4	5
15. How important is it for you to use a certain format to pray?	1	2	3	4	5
16. How important is your prayer life to the growth of the church?	1	2	3	4	5
17. How essential are your prayers to the ministries of the church?	1	2	3	4	5
18. How much does your spiritual growth depend upon your prayer life?	1	2	4	4	5

Evaluate your answers and mark areas where improvement is needed.

This form can be modified for your usefulness.

PRAYER REQUEST

FORM

Date _____

This form is for your prayer request. Please fill out and return to the prayer request box which is located in the Sanctuary. Your name is optional. **"The prayers of the righteous availeth much"** (James 5:16).

_____

_____

_____

_____

_____

_____

_____

Would you like to be placed on our Prayer Request list?

Yes _____ No _____

NAME (optional) _____

ADDRESS _____ CITY _____ STATE _____ ZIP

TELEPHONE _____ (   ) _____

Each prayer request will be prayed over during the following week of your request.

Please be prayerful with the prayer team as they intercede on your behalf.

The following is an example of a prayer journal. It can be modified for your usefulness. You may duplicate as many as needed.

SESSION #10

Design Your Prayer Journal

2. Prayer Journal: Journal Outline

Prayer concerns, needs, and issues

- Call no: 1. Date. _____ Concern: _____

  _____

  _____.

- Call no: 2. Date. _____ Concern: _____

  _____

  _____.

3. Task for both people.

- Find scriptures that identifies with your prayer concerns or the prayer concerns of the person you are praying for.

    (The concordance is a good place to start)

    Write these scriptures out. Scripture 1._____

    _____

    _____

    Scripture 2. _____

    _____ Etc.

4. Share these scriptures with your partner on your next call.

    Date. _____. Time. _____

Pass out prayer request to congregation. Suggested time is during or after the Worship Service. Also, check sick and shut-in list from your sick report. List their concerns and pray for them.

SESSION #11

Write a paragraph on what you have learned
from this section.

_____

_____

_____

_____

_____

_____

_____

_____

_____

_____

_____

_____

_____

_____

_____

_____

_____

_____

Now you are ready to evangelize your church and community.

We talk one to another we should not be afraid to talk to God.

CHURCH SURVEY FORM

DATE _____

Name:_____

Address: _____. Phone: _____

Martial Status: _____

Married: _____ Single: _____ Divorce: _____ Widow: _____

Number of children: _____. Membership: _____

Last time Attended: _____. Church Participation: _____

_____

Community Involvement: _____

How can our church be of service to you and your family: _____

_____

Would you like to see your children involved in church activities: _____

_____

What would you like to see the church do for the community? _____

_____

Will you help? _____ How? _____

Do you understand what the church is about? _____

What is the church to you? _____

_____

Do you read the Bible? _____. Read the entire book of Romans.

Provide those you witness to church and give them a schedule of your church services and activities.

May we pray for you, your needs, and your family? _____

FOR COMMENTS CONCERNING THIS BOOK, PLEASE
WRITE OR CALL:

JOHN HALBERT
338 WASHINGTON STREET
GLENCOE, IL 60022-1833

(847) 786-4209

If you are interested in him coming to minister at your church or organization, please contact him at the information above.